# Poems Verses Wor
## The first in the queue

# Poems Verses
# Words of Rhyme
## The arc of a learning curve

Jumpin Media
Books 2018

# Poems Verses Words of Rhyme

## A Pocket Book of Poems
### The arc of a learning curve

Jumpin Media
Books 2018

# Acknowledgements

With thanks to everyone and anyone, we are all as important as the next person.

Special thanks to me two sisters & two brothers, Mum & Dad, step Mum & step sisters, three adult children, one ex-wife and girlfriends, family & friends, and anyone who knows me or has met me, past and present, good or bad, happy and sad, experiences learnt and still learning.

Where ever I be, where ever I roam, you're in my heart, my heart of home. xx

Also a big thanks to KDP Amazon, in more ways than one, they help people put their written work into book form and help connect us to the outside world.

Jumpin Media Books 2018
Let the poems begin


## 'Our Planets'

Don't mess with our planets
Leave them alone
You don't mess with a dog
Once given a bone

Explore as you please
And wonder in awe
But don't mess with our planets
Not anymore

No drilling or hacking, into the core
Don't mess with our planets anymore

In place for a reason
Sphere orbs in afore
Don't mess with our planets
Not anymore

Upsetting the balance
Of all that is good
Thank Heavens the Universe
Is not made of wood

### 'Until the Weekend'

I like to wash you know I do
But wait until the weekend
A hectic life, even more a stressed wife
But I take a wash at weekend

In the tub and have a good scrub
To wash away the hectic
Life's distress can be a mess
And sometimes turn out eclectic

So to make things right
I may wash at night
But always on a weekend

The wife don't care
She's never really there
As both our lives are hectic

I take a brew, some biscuits too
And even a fluffy pillar
Then rest my head
Like the baths my bed
And dream of Aston Villa

## 'People see'

People see someone who's quiet
And reformed in their ways
A problem in later life
Only if gossip says

Others do not know
What is on their mind?
What the person is thinking
Or how this person behaves

Some people place a label
On a newly made bag
Even label a quiet person
With a tag
Not always a good tag, at that

Due to the lack of intellect
The lack of understanding
It's so easier to label a person
Than to understand, another person

## 'Area of Natural Wood'

Meander through a woodland
Trees of numerical shapes
Within a carpet leaf undergrowth
Bluebells air their grace

A gentle stroll leisurely by
Brush passed a conical shrub
One variety of shapely contours
You'll come through in a wood

A covering line of tall trees
The sun tries to push between
Yet darkness is still a bright
Casting shadows can stay seen

Do you see brown and greens?
Certainly some colours of a rainbow
There's beauty in wooded woodland
Appearances, be there deceptive

## 'A piece of Toast'

I love my toast, but not a lover of cold
A slice of normal bread
Shaped like a wedge of good cheese
Beholding to me please

Together with a mug of coffee
And neither a jam or a fancy top
An impartial buttered dressing
Will be eaten warm, if not hot

The burnt edges add some taste
And colour to an almost crisp
Crunch, the edges are by far
A saviour of the char

I don't do triangles or half a cut
A whole slice please, as it stands
I don't do one but maybe more
Abound my taste bud glands

It's just toast, innit'

### 'Don't begrudge'

I don't begrudge anyone making a living
Earning their way
Paying their way
We need companies to make profits
To employ more people

We don't need Fat Cats
They take all they can
Squeeze the milk dry, and why
For their own greed
Off the backs of others

There's such thing as too much profit
Too much greed
When others are in desperate need
Victorian times in the 21$^{st}$ century
Or near as

Wealthy continue taking
Poor just about making, ends meet
Poor man on the street
Fat Cat sat in luxury
From the makings of you and me

Fat Cat bonuses stay at the top
Do not work the chain
Down the staff line

For others to gain

The system works
If only the profits and bonus
Would feed down the line.
Other people would then spend
This means the economy
Would then work out fine

### 'Mr Fun-shine'

Throughout our life and days
Some of us look for a little extra
To have a little more
Than the neighbours
The person next door

We seek Mr fun-shine
Out of the mundane, the bane
The everyday pain

Some of us find an escape, another door
Another level, another floor
A way to work along the repetitive
Comfortable in the life we live

Others just continue
In habitual life, waiting, knowing
One day things will change
But when they do, will they be ready

All we can do is enjoy the life
We now have, have fun when we can
Not worry about how others live their life
Be happy as who we are
There is no big cigar

We seek Mr fun-shine

Out of the mundane, the bane
The everyday pain

Enjoy the time we are given
Struggling makes us that stronger person
Considerate to a fault

Look at life differently than normal
It's good to struggle
Stay in the groove
Take away the remove
For life will slowly improve
Time, will change for the better

## 'Lonely Bench'

I sit on a cold lonely bench
Looking out to sea
Lost my thoughts in the waves
Nothing much too see

Just reflect on life today
Could it be different in anyway

A thrash of waves appear fresh
Yet almost old, as tide comes into beach
Pushes my thoughts beyond reach
But still touchable

I sit on a lonely bench
Testing times ahead
Brave enough to live my life
Through the trouble and strife

A wind chill, waves that roar
Keeps my thoughts on the floor

A sigh of relief, beyond belief
Tide moves on, time is just the same
Will I sit on this lonely bench again?

## 'Blow me hearty'

Blow me hearty, wind and sea
Those soaring gulls in the air
Take a swoop, then a dive
Majestically, above they glide

Look out upon the horizon
Far as the eye can see
A lowly figure walks the shore
To a backdrop waves, a roar

Smell of sand and of sea
Saltiness in the ambience tone
Pebbled covering, almost carpet a beach
With a slight degree of undertone

A tide turns behind your back
As it almost wave's goodbye
Catch a glimpse of a moonlit sea
In this, a moonlit night sky

### 'That's Right!'

Looking forward
To all things good
On better ground
That I once stood
Nothing could be
So plain and clear
I am definitely going
To be here next year


### 'Chipped a bone'

Sat in my rented flat
Seated in my easy chair, nearest the window
The rain battering the panes of glass
In the plastic window frame

I glance up and look out
To a dull, misery grey sky day
The tree outside my window
Swaying every time the wind blows

I rest my leg on my waste bucket
Wrapped tightly, in a torn strip of old duvet cover
Held tightly together, with blue insulation tape
The sort of tape used for electrical wiring

With the help of some pain killers
I can keep the aching pain, to a minimum
As long as I don't move around too much
My leg feels fine

I may have chipped a bone in my leg
When I was riding my push bike
Out of the Supermarket car park in town
That was on Friday afternoon

It would be a waste of time
Going to the Doctors or even A&E
They are under enough strain as it is
Just to strap my leg up in plaster
For about 4-6 weeks

It is better to just carry on
Let my leg heal itself in time
As long as I don't move around too much
I think it should be okay

## 'Time Rotation'

I once stood on the sands of time
Inching slowly, steadying my feet
I came to realize the sands of time
Were never too be discreet

When all the time in the world
Could never change my course
Nor matter in the slightest respect
To all the thoughts I endorse

Sands of time, moments in time
Once gone are never gotten back
Unlike the damage in a vase
You can mend that broken crack

I once stood on the sands of time
This made no difference you see
As time itself stops for no man
That consists of the likes of me

### 'Boxed Soldiers'

Are we like a box of tin soldiers?
All dancing the same song of strife
We all address life so differently
But seem to be doing
The same things in life

On the outside it's hard to notice
Because of each other's false facade
On the inside, we all have similar things to do
In our daily lives, not realising

We are actually the same
In the way that we behave
Playing the living game
Going about life differently
Than to each other

We all seem to be programmed
Onto the same wave length
Acting like mechanical, minded robots
In the process, on the same fence

We are soldiers out of a boxed tin
Living life of similar akin

## 'Cycle, Pedal, Ride a Bike'

Whoa another pothole, whoa another grid
Another pedestrian jumped out between cars

I try not to pedal far
Not because of traffic or cars
Nor the weather, but age
Tends sneaking up on you
On days you don't expect it to

When I do manage to cycle out
It can be such pleasure
Fresh air, exercise, without even trying
The minute cycling out

So much to see outdoors, even though
We all busy around life
One way or another, indoors

Take time out, cycle out
No need to go far
No call to take the car
Cycle, pedal, ride a bike

Just a short trip, for a short while
You'll be back, with a smile of happiness
Of easy leisure, feeling more vibrant

Add colour to those cheeks
Face and rear
So cycle, be careful
Watchful and alert
Cycle

## 'Roll on roll off'

Pandoro rolled on then rolled off
They rolled in and stayed a while
Brought their trucks and their ships
Then rolled out without a smile

They left disused barnacled pillars
Looking saddened at low tide
That where once rope laden
Looking so completely dignified

Baroness feels to a once busy area
Of shunting Lorries, yellow coat men
Stocking boats with container wares
From a clipboard pushing pen

All that's left is the destitute
Silence is with exception for the gulls
Even the wind blows silently
As the empty berth majestically lulls

Such a vast open space
Has lain waste for too long
Listen to the cries of emptiness
To put right to this wrong

## 'Funny Pair'

I once said
What a funny pair
Oh my
What a funny pair

Twice the trouble
More than one
Dubious nicknames
Ruth and Ron

Still the same
A funny pair
In the game
Double your pair

Pair of aces
Up their sleeve
Low and behold
Who would believe?

Cards and decks
Are not for me
I'd rather have
A cup of tea

### 'Formative Years'

The younger generation knows more
Than we give them credit for

They are up to date
Modern and socially aware
Not only in life styles
But in street thoroughfare

They are not many miles apart
From where we use to be
Down the generations
Of any family tree

So give youngsters a shout
A chance to progress
Show they are valued
And not just bad press

### 'February'

Mostly known for valentines
One singular day of the year
To show we love our partners
With cards, gifts and chocolate too
Words of love and endearment

February the month of celebration
Of all that's romantic, dreamy
All that's love, the fondness
Hearts and kisses adorn one day
Never more so
Than in the month of February

Red is the colour
Cards are the written voice
Chocolate is the taste of choice
Roses are the flowers
All the symbols of romance
Love and adoration
All to say 'I love you'
To that special someone
In the month of February

### 'Alter-ego, hidden self'

Somewhere lurking in ourselves
Is another us
One different to who we are

Could be a singer, an athlete
Or even a fighter pilot be
Who knows, not even we know
Until our hidden self, shows itself

This could be through a talent
A simple act waiting to shine
Be that different someone
We all feel it inside

Do we strive for something?
Hoping, we could be someone else
Other than just who we are

There is an alto ego, hiding in our self
Like a double mirror image
A dead ringer, chip off the old block
Maybe waiting to be free
From you and from me

## 'Conflict' of words

A war of words, spoken in haste
Misunderstood by one
In a mind of information, overkill
Decipher the easiest explained

When taking in an overload
Words just disappear
Becomes a fierce tempest storm
A cyclone, of rage and fear

Calm down your conflict, boiling up
Knock down, the house of anger
Mere words are not of stone
But expression is the key

Delay the rhythm in the voice
Deter, those provoking reactions
Necessity is not a need
Nor conflict, an approach to action

## 'Conflict'

Conflict or the art of war
Not as pretty as a picture
Nor a painting hanging fast

But conflict is aggression
Burning tempers in the mind
Spoken in stories of the past
Could society ever change?
Those people that invoke
The actions of a tempest
When mere words, could be spoke

In a world of tough policies
Struggling by the way
Evoke a thought of conflict
In the work rest and play

Yet even I get angry
When something is unfair
But never use conflict
That I wouldn't dare

The thought alone is surreal
Any conflict should be wrong
My only Achilles heel
Are written in poems or song

## 'No Vote No Vote'

What's the point?
No vote no vote
Whoever wins?
It's the same old, same as

Money for the wealthy
Take while you can
Get what you can

Taken from the poor
To feed the rich
Just one big stitch, up
The books balance only one way
For the wealthy, their pay day

Nothing more, nothing less
That's why the economy is a mess

## 'It's an Intrigue'

Some people have an air of intrigue about them
Whereas others, you can read like a book
Same old pages, same old look

Those of intrigue, are newly written
Chapters, untold
For the daring and the bold

A base of mystery
Slowly unfolding
But still remaining an intrigue
To know more
In almost excitement
Relaying tales of folklore

In no doubt
Like a character within a book
All the intrigue is lost
The more you look

## 'Potted Sapling'

I potted a sapling
Nurtured over the weeks
Too big for the pot
He outgrew his plastic cot

I rehoused my shrub
Lovingly cared for its tender wood
Sang songs in awe
Until my jaw dropped the floor

Getting big with its age
It out grew once again
So I rehoused the fella
In a bed of golden yellow

I fed and watered him well
Clipped and pruned him so nice
Watched him grow and mature
More doubled than twice

Standing tip top and proud
A garden shrub of attraction
More appeal than allure
All to my love and care

## 'People Crowded'

As people
We need to communicate
With one another
That's how life progresses

Through generations to generations
Sometimes, just sometimes
We need space from one another
Too much hustle, bustle
Very people crowded
Can upset a balanced mind

Too much is too much
A step back, a step away
From society
For a short while
Brings body and soul
Back to reality
Back to healthy living

It's good to change habits
Sometimes less is better
And more progressive, in the end

Especially as humans
We need contact for life to continue
Overcrowded brain can be unhealthy

Silence is golden
But only in the right context


## 'Untitled'

There's no freedom of speech
There's always somebody
Over listening to anothers words
As they speak
Caching the buzz words so to speak

Then like a chain line
Words are passed along
From person to person, storing
Up the details of what others say

There'll be a time
When people talking in public
To each other, will diminish
And we all have to speak
Out loud, indoors

## 'Stanah Life'

Sat resting on a long wooden bench
A picnic table to lean on
Relax, in the heat of the morning sun
Beaming down on me
Like a laser beam picking me out

My body reacting, like my skin needs
The suns energy and stores it, for a later date
Recharging itself in the wait
Stillness and calm is all around
In this wonderful position, at Stanah

I can see out onto the River Wyre
Across the river, houses that look small
Boats that looks even smaller
Trees still look tall, but the size of a large shrub

I can see the fields and the tall trees
That surrounds me but don't close me in
I could sit here for hours
Taking in, the relaxing atmosphere

Just listen to stillness and the talking scenery
Away from the hustle and bustle
Of everyday life, the problems
The trouble and the strife

Sitting here in quietness, outdoors
Only the birds to listen to
The wind blowing through tall trees
Almost a magical land
That has not yet been found

As I head back to the real world
Maybe one day I will return
Never to look back again
Staying in a magical world

Just to breathe the fresh air
Feel the goodness in my lungs
Live a quieter life and at a slower pace
Maybe one day, I will return


**'The Wind & Rain'**

I love to hear to rain
Against the window pane
The rain, between the tyres of a car
As it drives the wet road
The rain hit the roof tiles
And run down the guttering

The wind blowing the trees
Dancing a slow dance
As the wind blows
The tree dance is swaying faster

As the wind dies down
The dance is slow again
I love to hear the rain


**'It is what it is'**

It is what it is
Like life in itself
No changes make a difference
Nor no amount of wealth

What will happen, will occur
It's just a point of degree
That all the working out
Cannot change history

So it is what it is
No reason or no rhyme
You choose the life to live
Today, next week, in time

With age we all grow old
With grace we get along
Don't worry about the makings
As there is no right or wrong

## 'Eon Times'

I've sat here for eon times
While the world goes lazily by
I'd look towards all the false signs
And the cloud forms in the sky

Yet wonder why life in itself
Shadows the dreams in my mind
When all the aspirations, disappear in smoke
And cannot forever be found

Nothing changes, nothing ever will
As I put my thoughts in fate
And beyond the call of age and time
I think it's gonna be too late

So I've sat here for eon times
And dreamt away the days
Lost in a place of solitude and hope
That'll change my dreamy ways

Eon times, eon times
Gone by without a thought
Relive a life over again
And change the reflections caught

## 'Run Riot, Run Amok'

Can one run riot
Behave without restraint
Shout, yell, and jump around
Splash the walls with paint

Feel free of all control
No guidance to lead the way
Run riot, run amok
From the speech that words say

Imagination can run so wild
Let free with a hand that talks
Escape the controls of normality
In the dreams that one walks

## 'A Wall'

Brick by brick, row by row
The pattern formation occurs
Looking somewhat new yet somewhat old
A pattern does unfold
Striking in colour, striking with awe
The toil and trouble of the workers afore
Transformation, re-generation
Of an area once rubble en dust
Now turned out

Into a pure sight of lust
**'Working Team'**

Mixed generations the crust of a team
Working together, learning from each other
Co-operating in the task involved
Performing as a collective
Striving the same goal
Each skilled in completing the call
From flagging to walls
Put the trust in the teamwork
To work out the plan
Bringing together skills, we know we all can
Get the job done at the end of the day
Worth our weight in gold
Of anyone's pay, teamwork

## 'Hazy Morning Greys'

A mist of authority blocks out the morning sun
Lowering on the rooftops, before the day has begun
An eerie silence, an eerie mood befalls
Not just daybreak, but even early bird morning calls

A mist of authority brings stillness in the hour
To even the tallest clock tower
Tree tops, rooftops, mountains once so high
They all disappear in a mist of sky

One big cloud of fog covering all that's tall
And lowering thinly to pavement fall

Slowly through the day, cloudy grey mist clears
Once a stillness abound
Becomes movement
Like life is waking up all around

A yellow sun peaks through
And the colour sky of blue
Once a grey and dull colour
Now becomes a burst of colour again

Colour of trees, cars, houses, people's clothes
Dispense the dull undertone of greys
On this once
Hazy morning day

## 'Red Planet Mars'

The Sun, a yellow ball of Hell fire
Brightly outshines any other planets
In our Solar System by far
The Moon is like a planet of ice
In colour alone, in the night sky
But Mars the red planet, is actually red
Mars is so much more
The star of the Universe
The Milky Way, of the Galaxy

Mars, with its dark wrapper
With aptly red lettering
There's a succulent thick topping
Like a crust of thick milk chocolate
Covering a silky caramel toffee
Nougat based chocolate bar
Universally the best planet by far
Oh what a planet Mars bar

## 'Rooftops'

Rooftops to Heaven or are they to Hell
You don't get a choice when you're unwell

Like a lucky pick not of your choice
When the raffle is drawn it's another's voice

And all that was rosy is now beyond belief
And all those dreams now lay beneath

Rooftops in Heaven or rooftops in Hell
Is there much difference, can anyone tell

## 'A Face'

A face, doesn't show what's on the inside
Any ailments, any troubles, we seem to hide

A face, braves to smile through any pain
Good at hiding any sufferers strain

A face, can tell a story without even speaking
Show signs of happiness, in a greeting

A face, is the first contact for your eyes
And the last in all our goodbyes

A face, of mankind, however young or old
Can express the love or anger, we all hold

A face is a live visual art form
And every day, we all get to perform

A face is a reflection of the mind
Without, the true person is hard to find

But a face is just a face, is it not

## 'Cold Frost'

What a cold frosty start to the morning
Iced car windows
Iced pavements and iced roof tops

A little rain brushed across the area
This all disappeared
As the sun fought its way through
Bringing warmth and clear skies

But lurking in the shadows
You'll still find
The bitterness and a cold factor

Waiting for anyone who dares walk
Into its path or for those
That veers off their route

A walk in the warm sun
Puts a briskness
Back into a mundane life
That may have felt missing
For some years
Or just needed awakening again

### 'Just Beautiful'

Like painted stripes of toffee
Look good enough to eat
Notes on a music sheet
String the lines, singing
As they move along to the beat

Two lovers hand in hand
Stroll gently together
Lost in each other's world of bliss
Magic in their eyes
Separates' them from their surroundings
As they engage in a kiss

That's the wonders of how happiness
Can take you by surprise
In a heartfelt moment
When you look into someone's eyes

## 'Money grabbing'

Today's world is a corrupt world
People ripping people off
For their own gains
Big and small companies alike
For the sake of their own pockets
Survival instincts
When one country cuts back
Others follow suit
Like a hungry pack of wolves
Grouping together for a kill
And then sharing in the rewards
Top fat cat getting his share first
No humanity in the world anymore
As people are out to get what they can
While they can
At the expense of others

## 'Envisage the path'

On crumbled pavement I strode
On to kerb edged tarmac
No potholes here as I stride
With a bounce in my step
Compared to concrete pavement

Tarmac reminds me of walking
Over a fluffy carpet, bare footed

My leading path took me
To the sandy shore
Stones washed up
By the incoming tide

I followed the shore line
My feet imprinting on the sand
As I walked, pushing small
Stones into my footprints

Making more progress
Walking slowly, than walking
A brisk pace
So nice to hear natural sounds
Wind, sea, birds
Appose to
Cars, traffic, machines

Envisage a path
**'Fort of thoughts'**

Forts of William and of Augustus
Succumb to not being forts at all
Although strong and brave
Are now the opposite
Beauty in the wildest of places

Take a stroll, a slow meander
Were your feet have never been before
Awaken, agitate
Stir up your rambler's blood

Thoughts of William and of Augustus
Can be wild and wonderful
At the same time bald and bleak
Interpreted on different days

Make your walk a leisurely ramble
Inhaling such ruggedness and coloured contours
Arouse, allure
Perceive such legends of old
Such legends that stood
In the names of William and Augustus

### 'Tied Down'

I feel restrained, chained
Held back
Kept from making progress
Kept from moving on
I feel stuck, in a rut
Held back
Kept from pressing forward
Kept from going gone

I feel time moves faster
As life does hold back
I am getting nowhere
And nowhere is going fast

I feel change, rearrange
Is certainly long overdue
Move on into the future
Leave behind the past

### 'If scenery could talk'

If scenery could talk
I wonder what it would be saying
To me right now

What do the trees say
In their woody toned voice
As they reach out to speak

What do the snow topped mountains
Say in their crisp voice
When they stutter in the cold air

Or the flowing river says
In its rippled voice, as it gargles by

Even the flora
Has a bright and colourful voice
As it dances in the wind

What would the scenery say?

## 'Little Pebble Stone'

It's just no ordinary stone
Small in size maybe
But big in stance
Standing out from the rest
A stone of authority
In your presence

Your multi-coloured complex
Your dark indents, back grounded
With a grey white undertone
A stone offering much more
Than just a stone would

A story could be told
From an artist's eye
So little pebble stone
Proud in the collective
You hold an importance
In your being
Amongst larger, much boulder
Overshadowing your path
Pushing out your might
In the aura you possess

## 'Racing Cars'

Cars chasing time, in each lap they pass
Hugging corners, so tight
They squeeze out every inch
Like a tightened trouser belt

Wheel spinning, a fast carousel
Burning rubber that smells hot
As smoke fills the air, in a lap
Timed to sheer perfection

Engines spitting out fire
Like a fierce dragon in flight
Striking with a roar
Catching a tail wind.
See the mighty soar

Oh the exhausted cars
Pushed to the limit
Mechanically tuned performance
Like the horse power, in a race horse
Knowing the best of a job
Is a job well done

## 'Splash a while'

I walk through a puddle
And hear the splash beneath my feet
As my feet just brush the water aside
Such a compelling sound
A soothing sound
As I slowly venture
Into my next stride
Taking my time
As I walk purposely
So I can hear the splash
Sense the beauty of the puddle
That you would not feel
If you made a full on dash

## 'Valentine Love'

I'll send you red roses
A few dozen to fill a vase
The finest colour red
Like on the planet Mars

I'll buy you chocolates
That taste of the heavens above
Like nectar from the Gods
For you my turtle dove

I'll put my heart in a box
Gift wrapped with a fancy bow
So when you open it
You'll know I love you so

All of these things
Are for you my valentine
I'll shower you with all my love
Until the end of time

### 'Voice of a wind'

I've never heard a wind blow
With so much anger

Like a battle cry, of a thousand warriors
Pushing forward in their quest
For better ground

With the sound of a howling Wolf
Exchanging views
With a roaring Lion

Suddenly, like a sore throat
With a hoarse voice
The wind quietens

Similar to sand dunes in the desert
Drifting on the wind
Or waves in the ocean
Ripping up a surf
Before the calm

Has the wind blown itself out?
Or has it just moved direction
To voice its anger elsewhere

### 'Magpie'

I see a lonely Magpie
Sat atop a tree
White black and blue
Beautiful as can be

You sing a mournful song
Looking all around
Happily building nest
For love, may be found

A flight from tree to tree
Searching looking high
A solo flight upwards
Into clear blue sky

I no longer see a Magpie
In a lonely lost flight
But beauty to behold
A pair in uplift flight
Oh what a beautiful sight

### 'Edible Mountain'

The distant mountains across the bay
Resemble the tops of a peaked sponge cake
Dusted in icing sugar
So pleasing to the eye
And irresistibly, inviting to eat
Or walk amongst
And take a small nibble as you walk

### 'The tides ebb'

As the tide ebbs back out to sea
It takes with it
All the negatives in my life
All the misfortune and bad luck

As the tide ebbs into shore
With a haste
It brings all the positives to my life
All the fortune and good luck

## 'Lazy Day'

A stroll for these over 50 legs,
Up and down the mount
Onto kerbed paving as I amble on
Then just walk enroute a ramble

Mild wind blows
A cool freshness in the air

A stroll in the warm hazy day
Taken at a leisurely pace

The beach of pebbled sand
Voices or owners calling their dogs
Against the voice of the sea
As it laps in to shore

Ocean so calm
You could almost walk on it

Everything has a strange stillness about it
Even though there is movement
Everywhere you look
It's a lonely feel to the world
One were you could
Be elsewhere, but enjoy life
Just the same
Beachcombing

## 'Phoenix Rises'

Today the phoenix rises
From the ashes of a stale life
From the rubble of dereliction
From all the lows in life
Today the phoenix rises
With a change in life due
A change to go forward
A change to bring in the new
Cos today the phoenix rises


## 'Glenfinnan'

Oh Glennfinnan viaduct
Arched towers of bricklayers art
Stand tall in mountainous scenery
Stand proud, in train lover's hearts
Oh Glennfinnan viaduct
Birds have a bird's eye view
Across the glens, in the distance
Across the green fields and the sky blue
Oh Glennfinnan viaduct

## 'The Garage'

The garage is calling
And I must go back
Back to the town house
And steal the show
Back to the life
I once lived and know
Back to the times
That once looked back
The garage is calling
And I must go back

### 'Cheese on Toast'

Cheese on toast
Cheese on toast
Never thought
I'd like cheese on toast

Hot or cold
On brown or white
Cheese on toast
With every bite

A tasty snack
All by itself
Cheese on toast
A toast to good health

Yeh
Cheese on toast
Cheese on toast
Never thought
I'd like cheese on toast

## 'Five-o'clock shadow'

Tis a five o'clock shadow
And the six o'clock line
Shape casting figures
Are moving over time

Graffiti signed the walls
Pictures formed a shape
Not the perfect ideals
You'd love or either hate

This pace of evolution
A face behind a mask
Interprets time and presence
That's all but gone and passed

A cold rekindling heart
Wakes from pictures of old
Streamlined from devotion
In written stories told

Keep life's air so fresh
And keep above the pace
Live a generous life
With saviours and with grace

### 'High hopes'

Those high hopes can be a reality
Be patient
Just hold on
Until the dark clouds
Dreams have gone

Stay steady
Stay grounded
Look to the stars
Join the dots
From Venus to Mars

Turn slowly, turn around
Listen to the voice
From the quietest sounds

Have strength
In life and today
Belief and balance
In every way

## 'Untitled'

You got to be kidding me
Tattoos, motorbikes, chocolate, rock 'n' roll

Spinning my life away with
Tattoos, motorbikes, chocolate, rock 'n' roll

Dancing the night along the
Tattoos, motorbikes, chocolate rock 'n' roll

Time is too short to keep the
Tattoos, motorbikes, chocolate, rock 'n' roll

When dreaming music of northern
Tattoos, motorbikes, chocolate, rock 'n' roll

In the end it's down to
Tattoos, motorbikes, chocolate, rock 'n' roll
Where you make your choice
And you make your call

## Our Statement

We treat everyone fairly, irrespective of their age, gender or creed. We respect others; we respect where we work and where we live. You cannot please everyone and we wouldn't even try to do, as it's not in our nature to make someone like us. That is who we are, nothing more, nothing less, that is us.

Jumpin Media

Books 2018

26920797R00037

Printed in Great Britain
by Amazon